KETO FO...

40 Tested and Proven Ketogenic Diet Recipes to aid your body Fight and Prevent Cancer.
BONUS: 7 Days Meal Plan

Brooke R. Wilson

OTHER BOOKS BY THE AUTHOR

PROSTATE CANCER COOKBOOK

BREAST CANCER DIET COOKBOOK FOR NEWLY DIAGNOSED

THE HEALTHY SMOOTHIE FOR CANCER

THE ANTI-CANCER SURVIVAL GUIDE

ANTI-CANCER SMOOTHIE

FOODS TO FIGHT CANCER

TABLE OF CONTENTS

INTRODUCTION

In the face of adversity, the human spirit seeks strength and hope, an unwavering resolve to conquer the most daunting challenges life presents. "Keto for Cancer" stands as a beacon of light, a culinary journey that embraces the power of the ketogenic diet to aid those in their fight against cancer. Within these pages lie not just recipes but a transformative approach that has the potential to rewrite the stories of countless warriors battling this formidable foe.

Meet Emma, a courageous woman whose life was turned upside down when she received a life-altering diagnosis. Amidst the darkness, she found her way to the ketogenic lifestyle, unlocking a world of possibilities in her fight against cancer. With unwavering determination, Emma harnessed the healing properties of the ketogenic diet, pairing it with an array of delectable and nourishing recipes. As her body regained strength, her spirit soared, inspiring those around her and sparking the creation of "Keto for Cancer."

Within these pages, you'll find Emma's personal journey interwoven with 30 meticulously crafted recipes, each designed to provide vital nutrients and support to those on their own path to healing. These dishes empower individuals to embrace a diet that not only fuels their bodies but also uplifts their souls.

Embark on this empowering quest with us, as we invite you to explore the life-changing potential of "Keto for Cancer." Let the power of food and resilience guides you towards a brighter, healthier tomorrow.

7-DAYS KETO FOR CANCER MEAL PLAN

DAY 1:
Breakfast: Avocado Egg Cups
Lunch: Cauliflower Fried Rice
Dinner: Turmeric Grilled Chicken with Zesty Lemon Asparagus

DAY 2:
Breakfast: Almond Flour Pancakes with Blueberry Coconut Chia Pudding
Lunch: Keto Tuna Salad Lettuce Wraps
Dinner: Salmon Zucchini Noodles

Day 3:
Breakfast: Creamy Avocado Lime Dressing (as a dressing for a green salad)
Lunch: Chicken Broccoli Casserole
Dinner: Eggplant Lasagna

Day 4:
Breakfast: Lemon Poppy Seed Muffins
Lunch: Keto Meatball Zoodle Soup
Dinner: Spinach and Feta Stuffed Chicken with Garlic Parmesan Roasted Brussels Sprouts

Day 5:
Breakfast: Avocado Deviled Eggs
Lunch: Broccoli Cheese Soup
Dinner: Lemon Garlic Shrimp Skewers with Baked Parmesan Zucchini Fries

Day 6:
Breakfast: Keto Chocolate Avocado Pudding
Lunch: Greek Salad with Grilled Chicken
Dinner: Creamy Tomato Basil Soup
Day 7:

Breakfast: Creamy Garlic Mashed Cauliflower
Lunch: Buffalo Chicken Dip (as a dip with cucumber and celery sticks)
Dinner: Keto Lemon Garlic Roasted Chicken with Creamy Garlic Butter Mushrooms

40 CANCER KETOGENIC DIET RECIPES

I. Avocado Egg Cups
Ingredients:
2 ripe avocados
4 large eggs
Salt and pepper to taste
Optional toppings: chopped chives, cherry tomatoes
Preparation:
1. Preheat oven to 375°F (190°C).
2. Cut avocados in half, remove pits, and scoop out a little flesh to create space for the egg.
3. Break an egg into each avocado half.
4. Season with salt and pepper.
5. Bake for 12-15 minutes until eggs are set.
6. Garnish with optional toppings and serve.

2. Cauliflower Fried Rice
Ingredients:
1 medium head of cauliflower, grated
2 tablespoons coconut oil
1 cup diced vegetables (bell peppers, carrots, peas)
2 cloves garlic, minced
2 tablespoons tamari sauce (or soy sauce)
2 large eggs, beaten
Salt and pepper to taste
Green onions for garnish
Preparation:
1. Heat up the coconut oil in a large skillet over medium-high heat.
2. Add diced vegetables and garlic, sauté until tender.

3. Push veggies to one side of the skillet, add beaten eggs to the other side, scramble.

4. Mix in the grated cauliflower and tamari sauce. Cook for 5 minutes, stirring frequently.

5. Season with salt and pepper.

6. Before serving, garnish with the chopped green onions.

3. Turmeric Grilled Chicken

Ingredients:
4 boneless, skinless chicken breasts
2 tablespoons olive oil
1 tablespoon ground turmeric
1 teaspoon ground cumin
1 teaspoon paprika
1/2 teaspoon garlic powder
Salt and pepper to taste

Preparation:
1. Preheat grill to medium-high heat.

2. In a bowl, mix olive oil, turmeric, cumin, paprika, garlic powder, salt, and pepper.

3. Coat chicken breasts with the spice mixture.

4. Grill chicken for 6-7 minutes per side or until fully cooked.

5. Serve with your favorite keto-friendly side dishes.

4. Salmon Zucchini Noodles

Ingredients:
2 salmon fillets
2 medium zucchinis, spiralized
2 tablespoons olive oil
2 cloves garlic, minced
Juice of 1 lemon
Salt and pepper to taste
Fresh parsley for garnish

Preparation:
1. Season the salmon fillets with salt and pepper.
2. In a skillet, heat up olive oil over medium heat. Add garlic and sauté for a minute.
3. Add salmon to the skillet and cook for 4-5 minutes per side or until done.
4. In the same skillet, add spiralized zucchini noodles and lemon juice. Toss until heated through.
5. Garnish with fresh parsley before serving.

6. Broccoli Cheese Soup

Ingredients:
2 cups broccoli florets
2 cups chicken broth
1 cup heavy cream
1 cup shredded cheddar cheese
2 tablespoons butter
2 cloves garlic, minced
Salt and pepper to taste

Preparation:
1. In a pot, melt butter over average heat. Stir in the minced garlic and sauté until fragrant.
2. Add broccoli and chicken broth, bring to a boil, and simmer for 10 minutes until broccoli is tender.
3. Using an immersion blender puree the soup until smooth.
4. Stir in heavy cream and shredded cheddar cheese until cheese is melted.
5. Season with salt and pepper.
6. Serve hot.

7. Lemon Garlic Shrimp Skewers

Ingredients:
1 pound large shrimp, peeled and deveined
Zest and juice of 1 lemon

2 cloves garlic, minced
2 tablespoons olive oil
1 tablespoon fresh parsley, chopped
Salt and pepper to taste
Preparation:
1. In a bowl, combine olive oil, lemon zest, lemon juice, minced garlic, chopped parsley, salt, and pepper.
2. Add shrimp to the bowl and toss to coat them in the marinade.
3. Cover and refrigerate for 30 minutes.
4. Thread shrimp onto skewers and grill for 2-3 minutes per side or until cooked through.
5. Serve together with grilled vegetables or a side salad.

8. Spinach and Feta Stuffed Chicken
Ingredients:
4 boneless, skinless chicken breasts
2 cups fresh spinach
1/2 cup crumbled feta cheese
2 tablespoons olive oil
1 teaspoon dried oregano
Salt and pepper to taste
Preparation:
1. Preheat oven to 375°F (190°C).
2. Cut a pocket into each chicken breast by making a horizontal cut along the side.
3. Season the inside of the pockets with salt, pepper, and dried oregano.
4. Stuff each pocket with spinach and feta cheese.
5. Secure the openings with toothpicks.
6. Heat up olive oil in an oven-safe skillet over medium-high heat.
7. Sear the stuffed chicken breasts for 2 minutes per side.

8. Transfer the skillet to the preheated oven and bake for 15-20 minutes or until chicken is fully cooked.
9. Remove toothpicks before serving.

9. Creamy Garlic Mashed Cauliflower
Ingredients:
1 medium head of a cauliflower, cut into florets
2 tablespoons butter
2 cloves garlic, minced
1/4 cup heavy cream
Salt and pepper to taste
Chopped fresh chives for garnish
Preparation:
1. Steam cauliflower florets until tender.
2. In a separate skillet, melt butter over a medium heat. Stir in the minced garlic and sauté until fragrant.
3. Transfer the steamed cauliflower to a food processor or blender.
4. Add the sautéed garlic, heavy cream, salt, and pepper.
5. Blend until smooth and creamy.
6. Garnish with chopped fresh chives before serving.

10. Coconut Curry Chicken
Ingredients:
4 boneless, skinless chicken breasts cut into cubes
1 tablespoon coconut oil
1 can (14 oz) coconut milk
2 tablespoons red curry paste
1 tablespoon fish sauce
1 tablespoon grated ginger
1 red bell pepper, sliced
1 cup sliced mushrooms
Fresh cilantro for garnish
Preparation:

1. In a large skillet, heat coconut oil over medium-high heat.
2. Add chicken cubes and cook until browned on all sides.
3. Stir in red curry paste and grated ginger, cook for another minute.
4. Pour in the coconut milk and fish sauce, bring to a simmer.
5. Add sliced bell pepper and mushrooms, cook until vegetables are tender.
6. Garnish with fresh cilantro before serving.

11. Zesty Lemon Asparagus

Ingredients:
1 bunch asparagus, trimmed
2 tablespoons olive oil
Zest of 1 lemon
Salt and pepper to taste
Grated Parmesan cheese (optional)

Preparation:
1. Preheat oven to 400°F (200°C).
2. In a large bowl, toss asparagus with olive oil, lemon zest, salt, and pepper.
3. On a baking sheet, spread the asparagus in a single layer
4. Roast for 12-15 minutes until tender.
5. Optionally, sprinkle grated Parmesan cheese over the asparagus before serving.

12. Garlic Butter Steak Bites

Ingredients:
1 pound sirloin steak, slice into bite-sized pieces
2 tablespoons butter
2 cloves garlic, minced
Salt and pepper to taste
Chopped fresh parsley for garnish

Preparation:
1. In a skillet, melt butter over medium-high heat.
2. Put in the minced garlic and sauté until fragrant.
3. Put in steak bites to the skillet and cook for 2-3 minutes per side or until desired doneness.
4. Season with salt and pepper.
5. Garnish with chopped fresh parsley before serving.

13. Spaghetti Squash Carbonara

Ingredients:
1 medium spaghetti squash
4 slices bacon, chopped
3 large eggs
1/2 cup grated Parmesan cheese
1/4 cup heavy cream
2 cloves garlic, minced
Salt and pepper to taste
Chopped fresh parsley for garnish

Preparation:
1. Preheat oven to 375°F (190°C).
2. Cut spaghetti squash in half lengthwise and remove seeds.
3. Lay the squash halves cut-side down on a baking sheet. Bake for 30-40 minutes until tender.
4. Let the squash cool slightly, then use a fork to scrape the flesh into "spaghetti" strands.
5. In a skillet, cook chopped bacon until crispy. Remove bacon and set aside.
6. In a bowl, whisk together eggs, grated Parmesan cheese, heavy cream, minced garlic, salt, and pepper.
7. Pour the egg mixture into the skillet over low heat.
8. Add the spaghetti squash strands and cooked bacon to the skillet. Toss until thoroughly coated and heated.
9. Garnish with chopped fresh parsley before serving.

14. Creamy Garlic Butter Mushrooms

Ingredients:
1 pound mushrooms, sliced
2 tablespoons butter
2 cloves garlic, minced
1/4 cup chicken broth
1/2 cup heavy cream
Salt and pepper to taste
Chopped fresh parsley for garnish

Preparation:
1. In a large skillet, melt butter over an average heat.
2. Add sliced mushrooms and sauté until tender and slightly browned.
3. Put in the minced garlic and cook for another minute.
4. Pour in chicken broth and heavy cream, bring to a simmer.
5. Let the sauce thicken slightly, season with salt and pepper.
6. Before serving, garnish with chopped fresh parsley

15. Greek Salad with Grilled Chicken

Ingredients:
2 boneless, skinless chicken breasts
2 tablespoons olive oil
2 tablespoons lemon juice
1 teaspoon dried oregano
Salt and pepper to taste
2 cups mixed greens
1/2 cucumber, sliced
1/2 cup cherry tomatoes, halved
1/4 cup Kalamata olives
1/4 cup crumbled feta cheese
Red onion slices for garnish

Preparation:

1. In a bowl, whisk together olive oil, lemon juice, dried oregano, salt, and pepper.
2. Marinate chicken breasts in the mixture for 30 minutes.
3. Grill chicken for 6-7 minutes per side or until fully cooked.
4. Let the chicken cool for a few minutes before slicing.
5. In a salad bowl, combine mixed greens, cucumber, cherry tomatoes, Kalamata olives, and crumbled feta cheese.
6. Top the salad with sliced grilled chicken and red onion slices.
7. Drizzle with extra virgin olive oil and lemon juice if desired.

16. Creamy Avocado Lime Dressing

Ingredients:
1 ripe avocado
1/4 cup Greek yogurt
Juice of 2 limes
1/4 cup fresh cilantro
1 clove garlic
2 tablespoons olive oil
Salt and pepper to taste
Water (as needed for consistency)

Preparation:
1. In a blender or food processor, combine avocado, Greek yogurt, lime juice, cilantro, minced garlic, olive oil, salt, and pepper.
2. Blend until smooth and creamy.
3. Put water, a tablespoon at a time, until the desired dressing consistency is reached.
4. Use as a dressing for salads or as a dip for vegetables.

17. Baked Parmesan Zucchini Fries

Ingredients:
2 medium zucchinis, cut into fry-like shapes
1/2 cup grated Parmesan cheese
1/2 cup almond flour
2 large eggs, beaten
1 teaspoon dried Italian herbs
Salt and pepper to taste
Olive oil cooking spray

Preparation:
1. Preheat oven to 425°F (220°C).
2. In a bowl, mix grated Parmesan cheese, almond flour, dried Italian herbs, salt, and pepper.
3. Dip zucchini fries in beaten eggs, then coat them with the Parmesan mixture.
4. Place coated zucchini fries on a baking sheet lined with parchment paper.
5. Lightly spray the fries with olive oil cooking spray.
6. Bake for 20-25 minutes until crispy and golden brown.

18. Keto Chocolate Avocado Pudding

Ingredients:
2 ripe avocados
1/4 cup unsweetened cocoa powder
1/4 cup almond milk
2 tablespoons of keto-friendly sweetener (e.g., erythritol or stevia)
1 teaspoon vanilla extract
Pinch of salt
Optional toppings: sliced strawberries, unsweetened coconut flakes

Preparation:
1. In a blender or food processor, combine avocados, cocoa powder, almond milk, sweetener, vanilla extract, and salt.

2. Blend until smooth and creamy.
3. Chill the pudding in the refrigerator for at least 30 minutes before serving.
4. Serve with optional toppings if desired.

19. Lemon Rosemary Grilled Lamb Chops

Ingredients:
8 lamb chops
2 tablespoons olive oil
Zest and juice of 1 lemon
2 cloves garlic, minced
2 teaspoons chopped fresh rosemary
Salt and pepper to taste

Preparation:
1. In a bowl, combine together olive oil, lemon zest, lemon juice, minced garlic, chopped rosemary, salt, and pepper.
2. Put the lamb chops in a shallow dish and pour the marinade over them.
3. Cover and refrigerate for at least 1 hour.
4. Preheat grill to medium-high heat.
5. Grill lamb chops for 3-4 minutes per side for medium-rare or to your desired doneness.
6. Let the chops rest for a few minutes before serving.

20. Eggplant Lasagna

Ingredients:
1 large eggplant, sliced lengthwise
1 pound ground beef (or ground turkey)
1 cup keto-friendly marinara sauce
1 cup ricotta cheese
1 cup shredded mozzarella cheese
1/4 cup grated Parmesan cheese
2 tablespoons olive oil
2 cloves garlic, minced

1 teaspoon dried Italian herbs
Salt and pepper to taste
Fresh basil leaves for garnish
Preparation:
1. Preheat oven to 375°F (190°C).
2. Sprinkle salt on the eggplant slices and let them sit for 15 minutes to draw out excess moisture.
3. Tap the eggplant slices dry with paper towels.
4. In a skillet, heat up olive oil over medium-high heat.
5. Put minced garlic and sauté until fragrant.
6. Add ground beef (or turkey) and cook until browned. Season with dried Italian herbs, salt, and pepper.
7. In a baking dish, spread a layer of marinara sauce at the bottom.
8. Layer eggplant slices, ricotta cheese, ground meat mixture, and shredded mozzarella cheese.
9. Repeat the layers until all ingredients are used, ending with a layer of mozzarella cheese on top.
10. Sprinkle grated Parmesan cheese over the lasagna.
11. Cover up the baking dish with foil and bake for 30 minutes.
12. Remove the foil and bake for an additional 10-15 minutes until the cheese is bubbly and golden.
13. Before serving, garnish with fresh basil leaves.

21. Almond Flour Pancakes
Ingredients:
1 cup almond flour
1 teaspoon baking powder
1/4 teaspoon salt
2 large eggs
1/4 cup almond milk
2 tablespoons melted butter

1 tablespoon keto-friendly sweetener (e.g., erythritol or stevia)
1 teaspoon vanilla extract
Coconut oil or butter for lubricating the pan
Preparation:
1. In a bowl, whisk together almond flour, baking powder, and salt.
2. In a separate bowl, beat eggs, almond milk, melted butter, sweetener, and vanilla extract.
3. Put the wet ingredients into the dry ingredients and stir until well combined.
4. Let the batter rest for 5 minutes to thicken slightly.
5. Heat a non-stick skillet over medium heat and grease it with butter or coconut oil.
6. Pour the 1/4 cup of the pancake batter onto the skillet for each pancake.
7. Boil until bubbles form on the surface, then flip and cook for another minute.
8. Serve with sugar-free maple syrup and berries if desired.

22. Garlic Parmesan Roasted Brussels Sprouts

Ingredients:
1 pound Brussels sprouts, halved
2 tablespoons olive oil
2 cloves garlic, minced
1/4 cup grated Parmesan cheese
Salt and pepper to taste
Preparation:
1. Preheat oven to 400°F (200°C).
2. In a large bowl, toss Brussels sprouts with olive oil, minced garlic, salt, and pepper.
3. Lay the Brussels sprouts in a single layer on a baking sheet.
4. Roast for 20-25 minutes until crispy and browned.

5. Sprinkle grated Parmesan cheese over the Brussels sprouts before serving.

23. Keto Tuna Salad Lettuce Wraps

Ingredients:
2 cans tuna, drained
1/4 cup mayonnaise
1 tablespoon Dijon mustard
1/4 cup diced celery
1/4 cup diced red onion
1 tablespoon chopped fresh dill
Salt and pepper to taste
Large lettuce leaves (e.g., butter lettuce or romaine)

Preparation:
1. In a bowl, mix tuna, mayonnaise, Dijon mustard, diced celery, diced red onion, and chopped fresh dill, salt, and pepper.
2. Spoon the tuna salad onto the lettuce leaves.
3. Roll the lettuce leaves to form wraps.

24. Blueberry Coconut Chia Pudding

Ingredients:
1 cup unsweetened coconut milk
1/4 cup chia seeds
1 tablespoon keto-friendly sweetener (e.g., erythritol or stevia)
1/2 teaspoon vanilla extract
1/2 cup fresh blueberries
Unsweetened coconut flakes for garnish

Preparation:
1. In a bowl, whisk together coconut milk, chia seeds, sweetener, and vanilla extract.
2. Allow the mixture sit for 5 minutes, and then whisk again to break up any clumps.

3. Cover and refrigerate overnight or for at least 4 hours until the chia pudding thickens.
4. Before serving, stir in fresh blueberries and garnish with unsweetened coconut flakes.

25. Chicken Broccoli Casserole

Ingredients:
2 cups cooked shredded chicken
2 cups steamed broccoli florets
1 cup chicken broth
1/2 cup heavy cream
1/2 cup shredded cheddar cheese
2 tablespoons cream cheese
2 cloves garlic, minced
1 teaspoon dried thyme
Salt and pepper to taste
Almond flour for topping

Preparation:
1. Preheat oven to 375°F (190°C).
2. In a skillet, heat chicken broth and heavy cream over medium heat.
3. Add cream cheese and stir until melted and smooth.
4. Mix in minced garlic, dried thyme, salt, and pepper.
5. In a baking dish, layer shredded chicken and steamed broccoli.
6. Pour the creamy sauce over the chicken and broccoli.
7. Sprinkle shredded cheddar cheese on top.
8. Sprinkle almond flour over the cheese for a crunchy topping.
9. Bake for 20-25 minutes until the casserole is bubbly and golden.

26. Creamy Tomato Basil Soup

Ingredients:
2 cups canned diced tomatoes
1 cup chicken broth
1 cup heavy cream
2 tablespoons butter
2 cloves garlic, minced
1/4 cup chopped fresh basil
Salt and pepper to taste
Desired toppings: grated Parmesan cheese, fresh basil leaves

Preparation:
1. In a blender or food processor, puree canned diced tomatoes until smooth.
2. In a pot, melt butter over medium heat.
3. Add minced garlic and sauté until fragrant.
4. Pour in the pureed tomatoes and chicken broth, bring to a simmer.
5. Stir in heavy cream and chopped fresh basil, simmer for a few more minutes.
6. Season with salt and pepper.
7. Serve hot with desired toppings if preferred.

27. Bacon-Wrapped Asparagus

Ingredients:
1 bunch asparagus, trimmed
8 slices bacon
Salt and pepper to taste

Preparation:
1. Preheat oven to 425°F (220°C).
2. Wrap up each asparagus spear with a slice of bacon.
3. Place the wrapped asparagus on a baking sheet lined with parchment paper.

4. Bake for 15-20 minutes until bacon is crispy and asparagus is tender.
5. Season with salt and pepper before serving.

28. Avocado Deviled Eggs

Ingredients:
6 hard-boiled eggs, peeled and halved
1 ripe avocado
2 tablespoons mayonnaise
1 teaspoon Dijon mustard
1/2 teaspoon garlic powder
Salt and pepper to taste
Paprika for garnish

Preparation:
1. Carefully remove the yolks from the halved eggs and place them in a bowl.
2. Add ripe avocado, mayonnaise, Dijon mustard, garlic powder, salt, and pepper to the bowl with the egg yolks.
3. Mash and mix everything together until smooth and creamy.
4. Spoon the avocado-egg yolk mixture into the egg whites.
5. Garnish with paprika before serving.

29. Buffalo Chicken Dip

Ingredients:
2 cups shredded cooked chicken
1/2 cup cream cheese
1/4 cup sour cream
1/4 cup mayonnaise
1/4 cup hot sauce (adjust to your desired spice level)
1/2 cup shredded cheddar cheese
2 tablespoons chopped green onions
Celery sticks and cucumber slices for dipping

Preparation:

1. In a bowl, mix shredded chicken, cream cheese, sour cream, mayonnaise, and hot sauce.
2. Stir in shredded cheddar cheese and chopped green onions.
3. Transfer the mixture to an oven-safe dish.
4. Bake at 350°F (175°C) for 20-25 minutes until the dip is heated through and bubbly.
5. Serve with celery sticks and cucumber slices for dipping.

30. Chocolate Fat Bombs

Ingredients:
1/2 cup coconut oil, melted
1/4 cup unsweetened cocoa powder
2 tablespoons almond butter
2 tablespoons keto-friendly sweetener (either erythritol or stevia)
1 teaspoon vanilla extract
Pinch of salt

Preparation:
1. In a bowl, whisk together melted coconut oil, unsweetened cocoa powder, almond butter, sweetener, vanilla extract, and salt.
2. Pour the mixture into silicone molds or an ice cube tray.
3. Freeze for 1-2 hours until the fat bombs are firm.
4. Store the fat bombs in the refrigerator.

31. Cauliflower Rice Stir-Fry

Ingredients:
2 cups cauliflower rice
1 cup diced vegetables (bell peppers, carrots, broccoli)
2 tablespoons coconut aminos (or soy sauce)
2 tablespoons sesame oil
1 tablespoon grated ginger
2 cloves garlic, minced

1/4 cup chopped green onions
Salt and pepper to taste
Preparation:
1. In a skillet, heat sesame oil over medium-high heat.
2. Add grated ginger and minced garlic, sauté until fragrant.
3. Add diced vegetables and stir-fry until tender.
4. Mix in cauliflower rice and coconut aminos (or soy sauce).
5. Cook for 3-4 minutes, stirring occasionally.
6. Season with salt and pepper.
7. Garnish with chopped green onions before serving.

32. Keto Lemon Poppy Seed Muffins

Ingredients:
2 cups almond flour
1/4 cup coconut flour
1/4 cup keto-friendly sweetener (e.g., erythritol or stevia)
1 tablespoon poppy seeds
1 teaspoon baking powder
1/4 teaspoon salt
1/2 cup melted coconut oil
4 large eggs
1/4 cup unsweetened almond milk
Zest and juice of 1 lemon
1 teaspoon vanilla extract
Preparation:
1. Preheat oven to 350°F (175°C) and line a muffin tin with paper liners.
2. In a bowl, whisk together almond flour, coconut flour, sweetener, poppy seeds, baking powder, and salt.
3. In a separate bowl, whisk together melted coconut oil, eggs, almond milk, lemon zest, lemon juice, and vanilla extract.

4. Combine the wet and dry ingredients, mixing until smooth.
5. Divide the batter equally among the muffin cups.
6. Bake for 18-20 minutes until a toothpick inserted into the center comes out clean.

33. Chicken Avocado Salad
Ingredients:
2 cups cooked shredded chicken
1 ripe avocado, diced
1/4 cup diced red onion
1/4 cup diced cucumber
1/4 cup chopped fresh cilantro
Juice of 1 lime
2 tablespoons olive oil
Salt and pepper to taste
Preparation:
1. In a bowl, combine shredded chicken, diced avocado, red onion, cucumber, and chopped cilantro.
2. In a separate bowl, whisk together lime juice, olive oil, salt, and pepper.
3. Pour the dressing over the chicken avocado mixture and toss to coat.
4. Serve as a salad or in lettuce wraps.

34. Cheese and Bacon Stuffed Mushrooms
Ingredients:
12 large mushrooms, stems removed
1 cup shredded mozzarella cheese
1/4 cup grated Parmesan cheese
1/4 cup cooked and crumbled bacon
2 tablespoons chopped fresh parsley
2 tablespoons olive oil
Salt and pepper to taste

Preparation:
1. Preheat oven to 375°F (190°C).
2. In a bowl, combine shredded mozzarella cheese, grated Parmesan cheese, crumbled bacon, chopped parsley, olive oil, salt, and pepper.
3. Spoon over the cheese and bacon mixture into the mushroom caps.
4. Place the stuffed mushrooms on a baking sheet.
5. Bake for 15-18 minutes until the cheese is melted and bubbly.

35. Lemon Garlic Butter Shrimp

Ingredients:
1 pound large shrimp, peeled and deveined
1/4 cup melted butter
Zest and juice of 1 lemon
2 cloves garlic, minced
1 teaspoon dried oregano
Salt and pepper to taste
Chopped fresh parsley for garnish

Preparation:
1. In a bowl, whisk together melted butter, lemon zest, lemon juice, minced garlic, dried oregano, salt, and pepper.
2. Add shrimp to the bowl and toss to coat them in the marinade.
3. Let the shrimp marinate for 15 minutes.
4. In a skillet, cook the shrimp for 2-3 minutes per side or until pink and opaque.
5. Garnish with chopped fresh parsley before serving.

36. Lemon Cheesecake Bars

Ingredients:
2 cups almond flour
1/4 cup keto-friendly sweetener (e.g., erythritol or stevia)

1/2 cup melted butter
16 oz cream cheese, softened
1/2 cup keto-friendly sweetener (e.g., erythritol or stevia)
Zest and juice of 1 lemon
2 large eggs
1 teaspoon vanilla extract

Preparation:
1. Preheat oven to 350°F (175°C) and line a baking dish with parchment paper.
2. In a bowl, mix almond flour, 1/4 cup sweetener, and melted butter until a dough forms.
3. Press the dough into the bottom of the prepared baking dish to form the crust.
4. In a separate bowl, beat softened cream cheese, 1/2 cup sweetener, lemon zest, lemon juice, eggs, and vanilla extract until smooth and creamy.
5. Pour the cream cheese mixture over the crust in the baking dish.
6. Bake for 20-25 minutes until the edges are golden and the center is set.
7. Let the cheesecake bars cool completely before slicing and serving.

37. Keto Butter Chicken

Ingredients:
1 pound chicken thighs, cut into pieces
1 cup canned coconut milk
1/2 cup chicken broth
1/4 cup tomato paste
2 tablespoons ghee or butter
2 cloves garlic, minced
1 tablespoon grated ginger
1 teaspoon garam masala
1 teaspoon ground turmeric

1 teaspoon ground cumin
Salt and pepper to taste
Fresh cilantro for garnish
Preparation:
1. In a skillet, heat ghee or butter over medium-high heat.
2. Add minced garlic and grated ginger, sauté until fragrant.
3. Add chicken pieces and boil until browned on all sides.
4. Stir in garam masala, ground turmeric, ground cumin, salt, and pepper.
5. Pour in coconut milk, chicken broth, and tomato paste. Bring to a simmer.
6. Cook until the chicken is fully cooked and the sauce thickens slightly.
7. Garnish with fresh cilantro before serving.

38. Keto Meatball Zoodle Soup
Ingredients:
1 pound ground beef (or ground turkey)
1/4 cup almond flour
1 egg
2 cloves garlic, minced
1 teaspoon dried oregano
Salt and pepper to taste
4 cups chicken broth
2 medium zucchinis, spiralized
1 cup chopped spinach
Fresh parsley for garnish
Preparation:
1. In a bowl, combine ground beef (or turkey), almond flour, egg, minced garlic, dried oregano, salt, and pepper.
2. Mix until well combined, then shape the mixture into small meatballs.
3. In a pot, bring chicken broth to a simmer.

4. Add meatballs to the broth and cook for 10 minutes until cooked through.
5. Stir in spiralized zucchinis and chopped spinach.
6. Cook for another 2-3 minutes until the zoodles are tender.
7. Garnish with fresh parsley before serving.

39. Keto Bacon-Wrapped Jalapeño Poppers
Ingredients:
6 large jalapeño peppers, divide into two and seeds removed
1/2 cup cream cheese
1/4 cup shredded cheddar cheese
1/4 cup diced cooked bacon
Salt and pepper to taste
Preparation:
1. Preheat oven to 375°F (190°C) and line up a baking sheet with parchment paper.
2. In a bowl, mix cream cheese, shredded cheddar cheese, diced bacon, salt, and pepper.
3. Spoon the cream cheese mixture into the halved jalapeño peppers.
4. Wrap each stuffed jalapeño with a slice of bacon and secure with a toothpick.
5. Place the poppers on the prepared baking sheet.
6. Bake for 15-20 minutes until the bacon is crispy and the cheese is bubbly.

40. Keto Lemon Garlic Roasted Chicken
Ingredients:
1 whole chicken (about 4 pounds)
1/4 cup melted butter
Zest and juice of 1 lemon
2 cloves garlic, minced

1 teaspoon dried thyme
Salt and pepper to taste
Fresh thyme sprigs for garnish

Preparation:
1. Preheat oven to 425°F (220°C) and line a roasting pan with foil.
2. In a bowl, whisk together melted butter, lemon zest, lemon juice, minced garlic, dried thyme, salt, and pepper.
3. Rub the butter mixture all over the whole chicken.
4. Set the chicken in the roasting pan breast-side up.
5. Roast the chicken for 1 hour to 1 hour and 15 minutes.
6. Allow the chicken rest for a few minutes before carving.
7. Garnish with fresh thyme sprigs before serving.

CONCLUSION

This book "Keto for Cancer" offers a transformative approach to nutrition that empowers individuals to take control of their health and well-being amidst the challenging journey of cancer. This groundbreaking dietary strategy, rooted in the ketogenic principles, harnesses the body's natural metabolic processes to potentially enhance cancer therapies and improve overall quality of life.

Through a collection of 40 tested and proven recipes, this guide showcases the incredible diversity and deliciousness of a ketogenic diet, emphasizing nutrient-rich ingredients that nourish the body and support its fight against cancer. From hearty and comforting soups to savory main courses and delectable desserts, these recipes not only cater to taste buds but also prioritize nutritional value.

Beyond the kitchen, "Keto for Cancer" seeks to instill hope, resilience, and a renewed sense of empowerment in those facing the battle against cancer. By embracing the ketogenic lifestyle, individuals can embrace a holistic approach that complements conventional treatments, supporting their bodies' natural defenses while fostering a positive mindset.

As you embark on this journey together, let "Keto for Cancer" be a guiding light, illuminating the path to better health and fostering the belief that even in the face of adversity, profound healing is within reach. With courage, knowledge, and the power of nutrition, we stand united in our pursuit of strength, vitality, and triumph over cancer. Together, we shall overcome.

THANK YOU

Dear Reader,

Thank you from the depths of our hearts for investing your time and trust in "Keto for Cancer." Your dedication to exploring the transformative power of nutrition in the face of cancer is truly inspiring.

Within these pages, we've strived to craft a meaningful and nourishing experience for you. As you've ventured through the delicious recipes, we hope you've discovered the boundless potential of a ketogenic lifestyle to support your well-being.

Remember, you are not alone on this journey. The "Keto for Cancer" community stands united as a beacon of hope and resilience. May the knowledge gained and flavors savored within these pages ignite a renewed sense of empowerment as you embrace your path to better health.

Your commitment to self-care and nourishment fills us with gratitude. Together, let us continue to triumph over adversity, one nourishing step at a time.

Wishing you strength, vitality, and wellness always.

With heartfelt thanks,
The "Keto for Cancer" Team

Printed in Great Britain
by Amazon

48625305R00020